BLACK WOMEN TALK

POETRY

First Published in April 1987
By Black Womantalk Ltd
Box 32, 190 Upper Street
London N1 1RQ

Motifs and symbols from:

African Traditional Architecture by Susan Denyer,
published by Heineman.

Style Motif and Design in Chinese Art, by Michael Ridley
published by Blandford Press.

Folk and Tribal Design of India, by Enakshi Bhavnani,
published by Russi J. Taraporevalla

The front cover motif is a commonly used Yoruba
decorative symbol.

Typeset by Contemporary Graphics, 20 Bowling Green
Lane, London EC1

Cover Design and photograph by Suzanne Roden

Text Design by Dianne Ceresa

Printed and bound by Cox and Wyman, Cardiff Road,
Reading, Berkshire RG1 8EX.

Distributed by Airlift Book Co., 14 Baltic Street,
London EC1Y 0TB.

ISBN 1 870400 00 3

Contents

I'm writing to let you know . . .   61

The women could be invisible . . .   79

Where do I go who do I turn to . . .   85

Being a lesbian . . .   107

While your face uncoiled its questioning arc against the sky . . .   113

Don't fear mi dear you are loved . . .   117

Contributors   135

Editors   143

Introduction

The publication of the first black women's publishing press in this country is a historic occasion. For the first time black women have had control over the entire publishing process. It is now possible to look forward to a time when our children are reading books in their schools that express some of their reality.

However, the route we have taken and the struggle we have had to arrive at this place bears witness to the odds stacked against us in making our voices heard. As was made clear in our first leaflet introducing the formation of this collective:

"As black women we experience oppression due to our race, sex, class and sexuality on a daily basis and this is reflected in *every* area of our lives". Our experience of bringing out this book clearly illustrates the economic and political realities we have had to deal with as Black women wanting a publishing voice of our own.

Black Womantalk was set up in 1983 by a group of unemployed Black women of African and Asian descent who felt strongly about creating the space and the means for our voices to be heard. A lot of work was put into finding out about aspects of publishing, finance, possible premises, printing costs, legal status and distribution. Some of us went on training courses in publishing.

Women on the collective were active and involved in other groups, projects and struggles — resulting in the pressure on time being a problem. There were difficulties in arranging meetings at times which suited everyone. Different women could take on different amounts of work, which caused imbalances. The collective was inundated by requests to participate in various event — the first Feminist Book Fair, conferences, arts festivals, workshops, articles and more. As the only visible Black women's publishing group it was hard to refuse the opportunities given to raise our profile and our issues. All this we took on while continuing the hard graft of doing the ground work necessary to set up Black Womantalk. In spite of all this, there was often a good feeling after meetings. Amidst the pressures, there was a sense of exhilaration in making progress.

However — all this took its toll. The frustrations of not progressing fast enough in our search for secure funding and getting bogged down in endless funding application forms added stress to our already pressured daily lives. There was never enough time to thrash out our personal and political differences. A core of women stayed in the collective while others dropped in and out, causing problems of continuity and stability which in turn led to more frustration and more women leaving.

Two and a half years ago — through a combination of exhaustion and low morale the collective was reduced to two women. We took a complete break for six months and then over several heart-searching talks in pubs, decided to scrap the idea of going for funding and to concentrate on getting our first book out without any paid workers. We had just enough from donations to pay the publishing costs for one book and we decided to go ahead with a poetry anthology. An editorial group was established through contacts with women involved in writing and the process of soliciting for poems began in September 1985. Again this was not an easy stage. Black women are not used to their writing being taken seriously, and we realized early on that it wouldn't be a simple case of advertising for poems! We held several open readings for Black women and slowly they were persuaded to part with their writings. We eventually completed the task of selecting the poems in January 1986.

By this time the editorial group — who were now also the collective — were made up of women in full-time work, squeezing weekly meeting into evenings after often exhausting days. One of us also got pregnant and had a baby during this period, and another got hepatitis after a trip home. With determination and support from each other and our friends — we learnt the technical and promotional side of bringing out our first book — our baby! It's been a long pregnancy, but we have finally arrived.

So many different women have contributed to this book being a possibility. We would like to thank *all* the women who have, at some point over the past years, been involved in Black Womantalk — the women whose vision moved them to set up this collective against incredible odds, and those who sustained it along the way. There are also many others without whose lives and struggles this book would not have been possible. We would particularly like to thank and acknowledge all Black women who never had the opportunity/time/environment to write, yet whose very existence and struggle to live and raise children with dignity in an environment of extreme hostility, provided us with the nourishment and strength to move forward and produce this book.

Finally, special thanks to Roz, Shaila, Barbara, Jackie, Meiling and Dianne for their support and involvement which has been invaluable in the production of this book.

The Poems

As editors we did not try to put together an anthology which could be seen as 'representative' of Black women. We know our diversities, complexities and differences. There is no one picture that truly says who we are. Neither did we see ourselves as 'experts' choosing the Best Poems. Instead, we chose the poems that moved us, taught us, inspired us, bonded us, criticised and challenged us. The poems that expressed extraordinarily what in our lives might seem ordinary — but pulled out of us and languaged — have power for us.

This is a chant to our ancestors, to ourselves, to our

children. A recognition — self conscious, of our need to value ourselves in our words. We are the chantresses.

The poems are grouped by themes which make up sections. The title of each section is a line from one of the poems which expresses the broad theme. Some of the poems could have gone in several of the sections. Obviously poems cannot readily be pinned down to any single theme, it was not our wish in grouping the poems together to limit their expression, but to place them in some kind of context.

"England, this land that had been no mother to her."
Our lives and experiences — as shown in the poems vary greatly. One experience we do share is the inhospitability of the 'Mother Country'. These poems explore the varied nature of the racism experienced in our communities.

"Ask me where home is"
Where can we call home? The issue of belonging, given the complex nature of our backgrounds and cross cultures is a difficult one. Where do we look to learn from old customs? How can we belong without access to our language or in a war torn country?

"Her child eye captured all this"
What is our relationship with mothers, fathers and families? This section explores some childhood memories and also looks at how we experience ourselves as mothers relating to our children or the possibility of children.

"The women could be invisible here"
Demonstrates some of the starker aspects of patriarchy.

"I'm writing to let you know"
This section tells of the need to confront, challenge and learn from those that have caused us pain. In this 'speak out' we assert our right to name the wrongs in order that we can gain the insight we need to move on.

"Where do I go who do I turn to?"
Although it is difficult to speak of our pain it is often harder

to face the contradictions and problems within our own communities. It takes courage to explore our insecurities and to acknowledge ways we have been unsupportive to each other, fear and the loneliness we experienced when we feel we have been betrayed and have no-one to turn to.

"Being a lesbian"
Speaks for itself...

"While your face uncoiled its questioning arc across the sky"
This shows how nature can evoke and change moods.

"Don't fear mi dear you are loved"
Takes us through the ups and downs, joys, sensuality and passion of being loved, in love or loving!

Da Choong
Olivette Cole-Wilson
Bernardine Evaristo
Gabriela Pearse

Black Women Talk Poetry

◆◆

Gabriela Pearse

Women
Black women
of different —
ages colours nationalities religions classes
backgrounds cultures . . .
have entrusted us their work.

Pulled from dusty history
dusty draws chewed envelopes tablenapkins . . .
Laying down words to record
    that we do not forget —
forget how much is different in our paths.

Each of us having innumerable battles
with monsters inside —
not to mention those outside . . .
Battles — small acts of rebellions —
    whole scale
downright
heroism and courage.

What were our grandmothers recipes?
How many continents do they span?
Our great grandmothers and mothers —
would they recognise each other?
Would they recognise us
as — 'us'?

These are the words
quartered, divided and whole
whose contradictions
line our souls.
Words of resistance
which in sharing
we move forward
claiming what is ours.

England this land that had been no mother to her . . .

Waiting For The 171

Jackie Kay

She said it had to be that way,
him gone and her still in Englan,
as the hearse passed
huge shiny and stately
laden with flowers carrying
some body's bright burden.
It could have been her old man
in there, his short wirey frame
lying under all that blossom
travelling in the fanciest car
he'd ever had a ride in,
it could have been Louis
eight years ago, his eyes
closed to the journey.

She said another one gawn I wish
I was going too her eyes following
the promise as it drove past her
slowly. Yes. she said turning
to me and catching the surprise
in my eyes. Yes. What's the use
of my staying on here? It's time
for me to go. My husband gone
before that he was sick. My
family in Jamaica but I can't
go there. My husband buried here.
I have to wait and go with him.
Years of waiting sucked in her cheeks
years passed away in this cold country
England, the milk the honey the dreams gone too
England, this land that had been no mother to her.

Untitled

◆◆

Roma Thomas

Black women,
Tall, short, fat and thin
bathing the wounds of this nation.
Caring for people who have hatred in their eyes
though their limbs are paralysed.
Black women carrying the deadweight of the sick
bending low to clean up the mess in the farthest corners.
Struggling to keep life going in others.
At the end of the time they collect a see-through plastic
      envelope
The women try to purchase their dreams with the contents
      of these envelopes.
Long days and nights, in their spare-time they return to
the homes they are trying to make.
Go back to bathe the wounds of men and children
crushed by the daily grind of oppression.
Black women exchange overalls and uniforms for Home-
      clothes
but not Home-comforts.
Tales of heartache are drummed out by others at a regular
      pace
but no time to hear her utterances, they fall on deaf ears,
tears are shed in lonely space.

Bus Stop

◆◆

Carmen Tunde

Waiting at the bus stop,
Good day,
Work,
Play,
Bus come,
Not mine.

What's that land pon my face,
Warm,
Wet,
Gooey,
Ahhh,
them spit at me.

Blood rise,
Blood boil,
From toe to heel,
through calf and thigh,
through belly,
through heart,
Arms and brain,
Blood burning red,
Anger flow,
Ah who spit at me so!!!

Bus move
And gone,
Look up,
Shiny glass,
No face to see,
Who hate me?
who humiliate me?

All alone,
Anger have no place to go,
turn to tears,
and spill,
and flow.

Tribal Girl

◆◆

Bernardine Evaristo

I am of the Maasai
I live on Mayers Ranch
My country is Kenya
Our village could no longer survive
many of us died
each day the tourists
come to visit
they take photographs
as we talk or dance or eat
for them, for this
we are allowed to live
on Mayers Ranch
I am of the Maasai
My country is Kenya

Do they shut the door when she comes to visit?
Do they welcome us into their homes?
Or is it only in print/in ebony that we are admired?
Do they care about her as they love the beads

that hang between her breasts?
Do they care for us as they love the prints
that they now wear and make their own?
Or do they want to stuff her/oil her/preserve her
as a beautiful work of art.
Her breasts bare to be fondled
as she stands in their living room
contrasting with the pale walls
forever silent
to be placed where they desire
forever silent.

Weep by all Means

◆◆◆

Avril Rogers-Wright

Weep by all means
allow nature
to take her cleansing course
bringing relief

So long as
unthreatened complacency
does not return. For what earthly use
is tears
to people whose land, sea and air
has been ruined
for the benefit of the West?
People Dying
long, slow excruciating painful deaths
from cancer
which thrives
from the fallout of nuclear weapons
Women giving birth
to limbless abnormal babies.
It's happening now
in countries
not taught in your geography
not written in your history
whose bits of culture
sleep
in your museums for show.

So cry to your heart's content
don't expect sympathy
for receiving the perfected weapons
For your wars
between yourselves.
They are quite safe, untouched
until intolerance overides

sane reasoning.
You see the big bosses
are very careful
about your well-being
it is necessary.

Weep by all means
only remember
it wouldn't stop
this final bid
of showing supremacy
the determined effort
to finish off
with cold-blooded calculation
the non-people
the so-called third world.

For once burnt out
by tears
you become sated
in other words
useless
voice muted
instead of raised in anger
you see
that has no earthly use
at all.

That kind of numbness
Leaves me on my own
counting my dead
as they increase
Increase by the minute.

Judgement

Meiling Jin

My poems are all jagged at the edges
because *I* am a woman
who is jagged at the edges
I speak only of what I know.

Our memories are like broken glass
rubbing over smooth skin
the glass pierces the skin
and splinters there
blood oozes out and gives birth
to a cry: long and silent,
a cry for justice.
It shatters the universe.

Our memories are like jagged glass
they betray you
they speak of racism,
torture, deliberate genocide and rape.

This is our hell
but yours is the next.

The white leopard shall stalk the streets
devouring everything in its path
even the hand that spawned it.
People will run before it falling
amid the stench of rotting flesh.
We shall fall and disappear
but the earth shall refuse
to accept your carcass.

This is *your* nightmare.

Shame Shame
everybody knows

your name
and your crime

I am a woman
jagged at the edges
no longer able to forgive
I speak only of what I know
I know the universe
moves in a circle
so that your deeds
will find you.

Anger

◆◆◆◆◆◆◆◆◆◆◆◆◆◆◆◆◆◆◆◆◆◆◆◆◆◆◆◆◆◆◆◆◆◆◆◆

Zhana

Anger.
Seeing red
Explosive
Volcano
Violence
Hit, hatred, danger. Destruction.

Anger is something I can see, touch, taste. It comes in many
forms, ranging from mild irritation to overwhelming blind
fury. Heart pounding, blood rushing, orgasmic anger.

The woman in front of me getting off the bus *too slow.*
Or the one behind me who tells me to hurry up cause I'm
    too fat.
The whitey who calls me names
When I'm on my way home
Down a dark road
Late
At night
And I don't fight back.
The ticket booth attendant who's obnoxious to my
Brown face
And I can't reach him through the glass
And I say nothing
'Cause I know I could kill him
If I could get my hands on him —
But I'm scared of the consequences of making a fuss —
Really,
Is he worth the trouble?
The woman who is raped
And I want to know
Why she didn't smash his face in,

Why wasn't she strong enough to get the knife away from
    him,
Why hasn't somebody killed him,
Why is he still walking around free,
Why don't women stick together?

Anger.
Hate.
Love.
Pain.
Fear.
Passion.

I love my anger. It springs forth from me. It is live energy.

The phone rings.
I've been trying to reach you. I had just the job for you — but
    it's gone now. Where have you been?

So many lies.

You don't have enough experience.
You're overqualified.
Your experience doesn't count.

So many lies.

I'm angry because I know you'll never hire me. I'm the
    wrong color for you, the wrong size, the wrong sex.
I have too much power.
You wish to diminish me.
Keep me waiting 40 minutes in your waiting room —
when you know I won't protest.

Anger. It's real.

Anger when I'm helpless, hopeless.

"I'll ring you next week", the man says.
When he knows he has no more intention of ringing me

Than Father Christmas,
Next week,
Last week
Or any other week.
"I'll ring you next week", he says,
And I believe him.

I hate this anger.
It overwhelms me.
It prevents me from thinking of anything else.
It suffocates me.
I walk down the street, being angry, thinking total obsessive,
Raging,
Barely controlled
Anger.
I am not angry, I am anger.
I have become anger.

The Perfectly Baked Cakes

Bekleen Leong

You're not black or white
you're YELLOW
"Perfectly baked"
From the middle of the oven
in the Chinese myth.
Well that certainly explains a lot.

Ask me where home is . . .

I'd Also Like To Say . . .

◆◆

Adjoa Andoh

ask me where is home — home is where i am not,
i can give you my address,
ask me who is family — family is nowhere,
i can give you blood relatives,
everybody wants the positive,
we're strong, we're growing, we're together,
well i tell you, i say yeah, i grin,
i say yeah we're together!
so how come this woman, who is so strong and so together,
    cries and cries like a baby,
so hard that she's dry-coughing crying?
how come somewhere inside floods up in snot and tears and
    she knows she's alone,
she's always been separate and she didn't want to be,
she never never wanted to be
my grandmother writes and tells me i'm her eldest
    grandchild and she loves me,
she never told me that before and i was so happy that she
    loves me.
is my father feeling what i'm feeling right now?
are we together in being alone?
is that together?
if i have a daughter what will i tell her about belonging?
where will i show her that is her home?
joan riley, i thank you for your words that people say are so
    negative,
because they were in me all the time and you said them
and they erupted and poured and festered out of me,
and i don't think they will help me at all,
but they are a relief.
how i feel now i couldn't sit comfortably, i couldn't lie
    comfortably,
what i've wanted to say all along is screaming to the surface,
 and i say to you, black woman as i am,

born and bred and infested in white britain,
i say to you
when people ask me where i am from and i reply
my father's from ghana and my mother's english
that is exactly where i am from —
nowhere,
my father is from ghana,
my mother is from england,
i am from nowhere.
there is just me here and i wonder if my brother feels the
    same,
how can i be ghanaian when i've never lived there,
eating foofoo?
i can't even spell it, don't eat it and can't prepare it.
speaking fanti?
i don't have the right accent to even pronounce my own
    name properly.
no — not ghanaian.
english?
look at me, i'm black, i'm not white,
don't tell me i'm english, i've heard too many wogs and
    niggers and go back where you came from.
where's my heritage?
you don't just pick it up where you can, you grow up with it,
    you absorb it,
i have absorbed no one's land.
slip into dialect for that acting role, the one i'm expected to
    know from my family,
what do you want — gloucestershire west country?
                        — bristol west country?
french, german maybe?
taking a blackness which fades in and out of my reach, but is
    never mine,
this is what i am telling you sisters in sisterhood.
there are people here who are floating in the aloneness of
    only themselves,
unique creation, unique growing up, unique
    circumstances,

who will cast out for their links,
who will swallow hard on their differences from everyone
    else,
who don't belong here,
who don't belong there,
who have family which doesn't feel like family, blood, foster,
    adoptive,
who have white voices, black skins and no memories
    decisively white or black,
just a blur of hurt and remoteness and times of clutching at
    a new revealed blackness,
a blackness which they can eat, but which won't quite fully
    settle in their empty stomachs,
and i am one of them.

World Geography and the Rainbow Alliance

◆◆

Meiling Jin

Peking is in China
As Kingston is in Jamaica
As Delhi is in India
As nowhere, do we belong
You and I.

And should we ever run away
Where shall we run to?
And should we ever fight a war,
Who shall we fight for?
You and I.

At the end of the rainbow
Is a country of goodness
If we form an alliance,
Will we ever be free
To belong?

Or shall we always be carrying
Our ancestors coffins in a bag?
Searching the globe
For a place to belong
You and I.

Part Of Me Is A Stranger

◆◆

Dorothea Smartt

Part of me
is a stranger to myself
Dead
to myself
I cannot hear the rhythm of my body.
Do I even know how to listen?
Where to start?
Somewhere
in my consciousness
the legacy remains.
In my songs?
How will I know!

I cannot hear the rhythm of my body.
My 'ears'
have been sealed
my lessons
have gone untaught.
Who?
will teach me
the faded memories that remain
the pool!
from the great ocean
that would have been mine!
There is, was a better way than this.

I cannot hear the rhythm of my body,
I am half-whole!
Who
were my people?
Where is my land?
I
can only look
in the faces of the people

and hope the reflection
is close to mine.

Distanced connections.
Or
will I 'magically', 'romantically'
find a truer me someplace!
I don't think so
it was hard work then
it will be now.

I am half-whole
and silenced by my own tongue
what
other language do I have?
I am forced to turn my back on you
I know that much
but it's been so long
I only feel
an emptiness —
or ignore it.

Can I begin to imagine what was mine?

El Salvador March

◆◆◆

Gabriela Pearse

March
last days of march
brittle white cloudy sunshine
Today . . . the day, Sunday
           that teddy bears have
           their picnics

Pick bones
scavengers red meat
picks dig holes for
bombs to eat.

Charcoaled heads
pavement pillows
lonely for bodies.
Bodies around square
rosary treaded
fumbling peasant
hand on cool bead.
to bead of sweat
upper lip anxiety
to breed contempt for life.

Daily bread give
to us the land
not marines
brutalised to land
and kill
    not forgive the sins of many.

Man fifty
weeps in terror
in a womans skirt.
Remember the coward too . . .

Cowed into in into . . . into . . . in
by cowboys shooting their
way to history
by film.
By passing, ploughing through
evicting, bulldozing
anonymous life itself.

Blue Notes For Billie

◆◆

Jackie Kay

Been thinking of this black woman
the doors that were closed to her
the places outside she had to sit
waiting
whilst some of her band
ate inside the colour of skin that allowed

and yet
she created all those women in
that voice that could surprise out a laugh in you
or pull down the pain in you

when she's in a low-down groove
I think of the women that came
before her —
the black women who had masters
and who scrubbed the low-down floor
and the women who come
after her —
the black women who have bosses
and who scrub the low-down floor

she takes me round my world
long since she gone
long since she gone

and I know
that black man hangs still
that strangefruit
on the paw paw tree.

the beat goes on and
the dream misses a beat between
each leaving and each loss
and then finds that note again —

'love me or leave me or let me be lonely'
those women who could be so independantly Blue.

Reach up and catch this note Billie
high up in that gloomy sky
hear this note dip down
to all those places we are scared to go
to all those fears we're frightened to meet
you went to those places
you sang through them and deep down into them
and you dreamt
and those dreams are on record.

On record.

There are so many voices we aint never
heard nor know of;
But I can see you Billie
your full lips kiss my dreams.

Her child eye captured
all this . . .

Some Nights in Brooklyn and the Blood

◆◆

Jackie Kay

I was pulled out with forceps
left a gash down my left cheek
and puss that took months
to dry up — I nearly died
four months inside a glass cot
the loss not mine
the gain for all time

she came faithful
from Glasgow to Edinburgh
and peered through the glass
I must have felt somebody
wanting me to survive
against the odds
she would not 'pick another baby'

she brought me up
on cuddles and Campsie Glens
Burns suppers and wild mountain thyme
Glaswegian humour
and all the blooming heather
the moors empty as after
the bloody thing out of the womb
what roads I travelled to get there

II

I don't know what diseases
come down my line
when dentists and doctors ask
the old blood questions about family runnings
I tell them: I have no nose or eyes or mouth

to match, no spitting image or dead cert
my face watches itself in the glass

pull it out — the matter
matted as unoiled locks
my dread needs some grease to shine
these way past midnight hours
when the loneblood takes me in Brooklyn

I have my parents who are not of the same tree
and my brother that is not of my blood
though he is my bloodbrother and
you keep trying to make it matter
the blood, the tie, the passing down
generations

I am like my mother and father
I have seeped in Scotland's flavours
sizzling oatcakes on the griddle
I am like the mother and father
who brought me up and taught me
not how to be black but
how not to be grateful
and for that I am glad

we all have our contradictions
the ones with the mother's nose and father's eyes have them
the blood does not bind confusion
yet some nights in Brooklyn
I confess to my contradiction
I want to know the blood from whence I sprang

III

I know my blood
it is dark ruby red and
comes regular and I use Lillets
I know my blood

when I cut my finger
I know what my blood looks like

it is the well the womb
the fucking seed
some nights in Brooklyn
I am far enough away to wonder
what were their faces like
who were their grandmothers
what were the days like
passed in Scotland
the land I come from
the soil in my blood

Manchester — A Childhood Memory

Tina Wildebeest

Piccadilly — My mother
Peering into Paulden's window display
I was three years old,
I had developed a habit
of hanging onto her —
Coat.
It was grey with bright, bold, yellow checks —
the height of fifties fashion.
Moving on,
I trotted happily behind her
until the ominous bulk
of the Emporess of India
blocked out the sun.
Speechless with terror
I tugged on the coat for reassurance
and a strange face
peered dumbly into mine.

I was too young to understand,
the meaning of Mass Production.

Memory Track

◆◆

Jackie Kay

It's Saturday she's putting her track
suit on, her brand new running shoes
spikes spark, she warms up
crabs stretches burpies and the lot
raring to go her fingers rest on red.

Her spikes stick to seven
sitting on her mammy's knee
watching the black and white TV
Cowboys and Indians
this time it's different
— all she sees is colour
"Why aren't you the same colour as me?"
"I am not your real Mother."

It felt like puff puff
blow your house down
was she plastic if she wasn't real then?
Who is the Real Mother

"I love you precious, it doesn't matter
that I'm not your real mother,"
the house was still standing
red-brick house

her mother holding her
solid as her feet on the track
her love had lapped years
— first true pal
she crouches into memory
then

fingers taut on the red gravel
she pushes her body upwards
and springs

My Mother's Hands

Dorothea Smartt

My hands are softer.
My Mum has hard hands.
Hard-working hands.
Her strength is in those hands.
Her love for us
I've felt those hands, in my hair, on my skin.

There is a softness in my mother's hands
that's nothing to do with how hard her skin is
elegant fingers with strong curved nails.

When I was younger, I'd do full manicures for her.
Buy her creams for her hands.
Soak her nails in oil.
Caress her hands, massage their vitality.

Smiling she would 'let me' trim and file,
then protest when I wanted to varnish them.
Smiling she would let me.
Her arm extended,
she would examine my 'thank you'.

After a night at work,
in the morning, as I helped her unpack the shopping,
I'd see that the colour had chipped,
and look at her hands in mine.

First Snow

◆◆

Zeina Carrington

Its nearly Christmas now
the memories flooding back
of last Christmas
when she died.

They force themselves
dark images
upon an eggshell shield
makeshift wall
veil-like black
and sapped with grief

Its almost Christmas now
days grow cold and
crystal
sharp clean and fresh
December soon is here
and shadows of attempted waisted
amnesia
fatigued with effort to forget

Its almost Christmas and
people-children
old and young will wager
for the want of
christmas white
first snow

Christmas will be upon us
will shroud us with the festive
and the snow
first flutters
feather flakes
floating upon us with our fear

tauntings of the morbid
tearing at our conscience
dragging at our hearts
to break again
beside that grave
where felt we on our cheeks
first snow of the year

For Christmas and
for her

(our mother)

Its nearly Christmas now
soon will come first snow

A Father's Passing and Sunset

◆◆

Dinah Butler

carry
rises
wake of
jagged edged
uneasy
darkening
descending
sun
our eyes eclipse
in acknowledgement
my sorrow seeps
with the bronzing out
of your primrose
full day shining
weighty yellow that
I clam and close
to own
dusk drops loss
disbelief hovers me
bereft
phantomed from darkness
shadows shape you a face
hollowed eyes
hollow me
scorch the tension
of my cold backed retreat
until it shatters for you
into distance
behind is that stain
of a relic
your photograph
mocks my wordless call
stretching a retching

to your unmove
that pulls up my tears
as your remembrance flowers
it cannot be changed
but still I ask
defy all
and give me peace

For Papy

◆◆◆

Adjoa Andoh

when someone says sad to me, i see my dad's eyes,
my dad loves words,
in ghana he was a journalist
come independance he became a journalist who used the
   wrong words
who wouldn't join the party
so who instead joined the isolated overseas
england is not ghana.
we sat in the pub my dad and me and i asked him about
   when he had come to england,
 about his last days in ghana,
when his friend went to prison and he fled the country.
his eyes drift somewhere else while his voice echoes their
   pain,
i wonder what it was like to be an unemployed exiled black
   journalist in england twenty six years ago,
and my tears are for all our shattered dreams and burnt
   illusions,
especially for my dad who lives alone, in a white country
   village,
and who is no longer a journalist.

Motherlove

Sylvia Parker

In one corner of the room
a woman sits
my mother
As a child
beaten
abused

She grew strong
Strong enough to beat me worse
And now I am strong
And with my child
I fight inside
to spare the rod

In one corner of the room
a woman sits
my mother
for whom I have felt hate
distrust
The rod with which I was beaten
hardened
and became her eyes
and her voice
And now as she smiles
It is still difficult
to remove from my thoughts
the memory of the lash
on my back
and the harshness and cruelty
of the hardness in her voice
and her eyes . . .

Perhaps
it was not possible

at that time
to hug
and cuddle
two dark girl children.

My Grandmother — The Bluebottle

Bekleen Leong

The Chinese goddess rears her head again;
(I did not say it was ugly
though some might think so).

What made me think this
was my grandmother
A bluebottle
Buzzing around
Rubbing her legs together in glee
Watching us make constant
mockeries of ourselves;

She knows
and can see
that however we choose
to spend our mortal days
We too will end up like She-
rubbing, or buzzing
or humming in glee.

Her First Toy

Sylvia Parker

I thank you for saving her life
my child
I really do
But did you have to give her
as her first toy
a white
doll

You think I am insincere
ungrateful
incapable of thanking you
But at this time
There is nothing big enough
to wipe away our difference
There is nothing
to bring us together
which does not leave a scar
the wounds as you see
are gaping

I thank you for saving her life
my child
I really do
But I wish you did not give her
as her first toy
a white
doll.

Baby

Dr Debjani Chatterjee

Your wobbly head was brown and bald — like Gandhi's.
Your clear eyes stared below Monalisa brows,
They smouldered strange green fires of innocent joy.
You sucked away, determined, at Daddy's pipe
And, frowning, lifted the rustling newspaper
In tightly clenched and dimpled hands, upside down.
Mummy's spectacles, so intellectual,
Perched on naughty nose, a little lopsided.
They gave you an air of owlish confidence.
You were seated in splendid solemnity
In crosslegged concentration on the floor,
Then toe in tiny mouth, huggable yogi!
Baby, how impatient you were to grow up!
Even while we watched our infant terrorist,
Astride the fierce tiger of our alsatian,
Opening grandpa's snuff-box on snowy bed,
Swallowing wriggly creatures in the garden,
Unafraid, reaching out for the stuff of life,
We could sense, little lady, you were destined
To always rule our world's inner circle.

C'mon Jesse

Adjoa Andoh

ha! she's asleep!
the cry that crosses days and nights.
ha! she's asleep!
hurtle downstairs to the bathroom for a shit — push!
time for a bath?
nah, better not risk it — settle for a wash eh.
ha! she's asleep!
start those letters, fill in the accounts,
do some writing, pay those bills.
ha! she's asleep!
i don't mind if she wakes up, she can cry on the tube,
of course i'll breast feed her!
well, what do you want me to do — let my daughter starve to
    death?!
ha! she's asleep!
ah leave it! put your feet up!
time for a cig, a beer, dynasty!
ha! she's asleep!
please don't wake up again,
if i don't get some sleep soon i'll die . . .
oh? she's asleep.
c'mon jesse, wake up! — i want to play now!
honestly! some babies are SO boring . . .

I Long To Be Pregnant

Carmen Tunde

I long to be pregnant
I want to love
a child
and care,
she cares for me
and grows,
she learns.

Through trials
and tribulations
we pass,
talking,
not talking,
hugging,
not hugging.

Her vulnerability
restricts my movements,
she is responsibility,
I'm frustrated,
I'm angry
at this world
at other women.

She starts to talk,
begins to walk,
she reads a book,
she disagrees,
she stays out late,
I worry.

We see a film,
we're friends,
caring company,
sisters.

I am not pregnant,
I don't fancy artificial insemination,
or a casual screw,
Don't want a man.

The birth certificate would read
'Father unknown'
and disapproval
hails on me.

Sisters assure
'shared responsibility'
until she's grown,
Can I trust . . .
that much?
Am I strong enough on my own?
Do I want to be?

Anyway,
How can I say,
I want this day,
When now
I have two children
not born of me,
Two and three,
Boy and girl,
Loving and lively,
But oh . . . so draining,
No time to write,
No time to sing.

My lover says
they're still in my care
if our relationship changes,
Can I trust . . .
that much?

I'm writing to let you know . . .

An Open Letter

Patricia Hilaire

Dear Man,
  I am writing to let you know
  that I'm a woman, now
  to remind you of the scars you gave
  me, left me
  to remind you of the nights I cried
  to remind you that I was not your bride
  to remind you that I was a total stranger
  to remind you that my mother was your wife
  to tell you that I'm taking you to court
  to tell you that the charge is
  RAPE . . .

  I hated myself for what you did to me
  I hated those parts of you in me
  and the promises you made me keep
  'blackmail' . . . childmail . . .
  male
  male
  male
  fear . . . on me
  a little little girl
  was I
  did mummy never wonder where I was?
  what lies did you tell her?
  what lies must I tell her this time?
  how will you stop her this time?
  from lashing me, beating me, shouting up on me?
  how will you stop her this time and the next
  and the next
  and the next
  and the
                the . . .

Dear Man,
   I'm writing to let you know
   that I'm alive and well
   that my body is well
   but my mind . . . is . . . mind . . . is . . .

Dear Man,
   I'm not out of my mind
   No, I'm in my mind
   yes, in my . . . mind
   and . . . not . . . going . . . mad . . .
   I'm not insane
   so don't laugh in my face
   or smile your gold teeth at me

Dear Man,
   I'm telling everyone,
   everything
   all the times
   all the nights
   all the pain
   the hurt, the smell, the sweat all the all the . . .

Dear Man,
   She's always known
   I know she's known
   the belt told me so
   her eyes told me so
   her voice
   her face
   her hands
   they told me over and over again
   and I felt it so
   I felt it

The day she kept me from school
in your bedroom
she tried to kill me
she lashed me

she scorned me
she speak up on me
because of you man
because of you
she told me so

Dear Man,
   I am writing to let you know
   that I'm a woman now
   to remind you that I was a child
   and my mother was your bride
   to remind you . . .
   to remind you . . .
   to remind you . . .

Dear Man,
   I just hope that you are
   alive and well
   for the charge I bring to you
   cannot be dropped
   for in me there's a place waiting
   to be set free
   but you still have the key
   you are holding my key
   and I want it
   my being depends on it
   and your life will be no more
   once I have my key
   your being
   your life
   will be put to rest
   as I take flight
   your spirit will never
   return

Dear Man,
   I write to remind you
   that the charge is
   R A P E

The Beast

B.B. Samuel

sack of nothing
feeling no movement no resistence no nothing
And wait

                    For THE BEAST

Is a shape
Dark mass of quivering flesh
Smells of cheap gin, cheap women

                    The Beast

Is of the night
storming through the house
Oppressive footsteps heavy on the stairs
Loud thumping at the door
Wrecks havoc with my peace

                    And

Tears the flimsy cover from my shame
Have you ever seen a head so purple,
throb, throb, throbbing with rage
A Shaft big and long and hard

                  violates my soul
But pain is not exquisite

A squashed pumpkin,
bruised and wet spewing revolting seed
A foul stench, perfume to

                    The Beast

will return
Tonight, and thereafter, after there
who really cares
Till death do us part
Beauty and

                    The Beast

'Tis no fairy tale.

A Second Wife

B.B. Samuel

I will not smile
Lest he thinks all is well
I will not laugh
Lest the world laugh at me
I will not see the sunrise
Lest the day feels I condone it
I will not hear the cock crow
Sweet smell of
Frying bean cakes
in the morning
Woe
Unto the day is breaking

I will not see the joy
On the children's faces
As they hit
Ripe Mangoes from the trees
With no sticks and stones
I will not cook
Maybe my husband will starve
If he beats me
I will not flinch

I will not
rub down the walls
and floors
of the hut

Wretched bridal hut
No red mud
from the stream
Shall stain my hands

I shall not lay the bed
where I once slept

Not quite five moons past
New white sheets
Bought last market
Let her lay her head

Who shall wash the dust
From her feet
As she enters the compound
Not I
I do not welcome
this
Usurper to my throne
my cooking pots
nor
my spoons
My fire place
is mine
These I will not share

No Regrets

◆◆

Patricia Hilaire

"Hay brown girl
wit yu woman liba ways
dont forget yu culture
black yu is black
now how you feel bout dat
yu can't pretend yu white
yu should know by now, dat ain't right
all we want is yu loyalty to de race
support yu brothers
we dont want yu white feminist way's"

So brother, afraid of my black feminist way's?
Afraid of my vocal range?
It's alright to fight the race war
when we dealing with the white racist
but when we get together, race becomes
second in line to the black sister
and our womanism takes the first place.

'Yu can't go on like dat sister
we hev to pull together
a woman mus stan by her man side
yu going on like yu wan fight me
bout womanism
next you'll be telling me bout
lesbianism"

Listen, if I wan to stand by anybody side
please let me hev the choice.

'But tell me, is wha goin happen when yu
wan a sweet dance?
Yu going wan me den"

No, not really.
You see, if I want to rock to the soul
or groove to jazz funk
my sister will join me, so leave the floor.
Oh, you think when the lovers rock hit the floor
I going to want you?
Well you jus watch how we hold the floor.

"Gowan wit yu woman way's
see how far yu getting without me . . .
wotless bitch!"

Think of your approach
you dont own me
and na bother raise yu hand fe hit me
cause you never born me!!

Yu black woman go-wan
yu is devisive . . .
yu ah go regret it . . .
'cause yu can't manage widout we . . ."

It's true you dont know
and is a pity you dont know . . .
why you dont jus stop there and
watch, see how we manage
widout you . . .

Seduction

Sylvia Parker

He
professing concern
with the women's cause
the black cause
the blackwomen's cause
in some fashion
seduces her
beds her
she
curls up
holding on to the warmth
sordid daylight
strips off the sheets
evidence-bare and tangled-
with its own scent
sordid daylight
turns gold and dusty pink
to crumbling ash
and yet she tries to hold on to the warmth
no longer a challenge
all mysteries unfold
as her flesh
He
becomes familiar
She retreats
not liking to be called 'darling' babe'
He
hands familiar
strokes dark flesh
She retreats
the locks
so beautiful
she wishes medusalike

so she could turn
this man
to stone

Missing You
◆◆

Sylvia Parker

I could miss you
like a lover would miss you
or like a friend would miss you
but I was neither

I could remember you
with joy
recall times spent together
but we never shared anything

I can only miss you
and remember you
as someone
who for a while
resembled the sun
and rushed about my soul
leaving a trail of fire
as someone
who for a while
resembled a stream
and washed me
of any illusions i had
about myself

You Leave

Sylvia Parker

You leave me like a fledgling
Wings fluttering weakly, ineffectually
hopelessly dependent on you

I do not know that I like this state
of affairs

You leave me like a broken puzzle
Only you have the perfect picture of me
I see myself reflected in your face

I do not know that I like to be
this helpless

You leave me
My life stored safely in your back
pocket
If you stumble I fall

You leave
I sit and wait with music and wine
Listen for footsteps and a jangle
of keys

I do not know that I like to be this alone

Fragile

Zeina Carrington

And you would treat
butterfly wings
with care
Clean leaves of
green with
loving delicacy
handle favourite objects
with the fondness of a
father . . .

so to help you understand
that I am
more unique than
complex flimsy
spiderwebs

I packaged myself
in a cardboard box
a picture of a glass
enscribed on the
outside

Because I break
more easily
and you do not notice
my pieces that you
tread on

For you to get the message and
stay unconscious that I am
Fragile;-
"HANDLE WITH CARE" though
what you crush cannot
be repaired

It just remains there
          remains
to show where your foot
once trod
like footprints in mud.

Insen (si mi) lia

◆◆

Tina Wildebeest

Lying face down
in a darkened room,
my thoughts
turning softly
like pages
in a Medieval
story book;
A strange
and silent world
opened up
before me,
each chapter
Revealing
embroidered,
fabled images
of the life
I was about
to embrace.
Unspoken quests
were woven
round my

unresisting body
in muted tones
of tapestry.
There was no threat —
UNTIL YOU ENTERED
and tried
to unsnarl
each silken strand
with strident chords
of senseless
laughter.
NO THREAT —
until I tried
to take back
the space
you had stolen
from me.
The only THREAT
lay in your
incapacity
to Understand!
Eventually,
when you had
Harangued me
and taken
my very freedom,
YOU SLEPT!
Deeply and Soundly,
leaving me
alone
in the night,
Whilst my body —
Which was no longer mine —
began to spin
uncontrollably
on a cross
of polished Ebony.

Abortion Is Not The Easy Option
Don't Assume

◆◆

Adjoa Andoh

mr r..................., gynaecological consultant,
purpose of examination,
you talked of counselling and sympathetic listening,
you were not sympathetic,
you did not counsel,
you were immediately aggressive, in much the same way as
    the games master
reprimanding the boy, who at the crucial moment,
drops the cricket ball.
wednesday 10 -day before my abortion,
it is insidious — within these hospital confines i refer to it as
'the termination'
bullshit,
it is antiseptic here,
and the bleak mint green makes the calm warm deadness —
    calmer,
i forgot that this was london,
and that most of the nursing staff would be black,
their silence speaks of disapproval and of a weariness at
    their work,
we are here — three women by our beds,
army fashion, awaiting our chief officer, the doctor,
the mythical man who is late,
we are punctual, they are always late,
the mythical man turns out to be a woman and is gentle and
    reassuring,
i am pleased.
night before my operation, my termination, my abortion,
tomorrow i attend the funeral of my non-baby baby,
i shall wear black and not face the experience with
    equanimity.
the day — my brother brought me in and i was tearful,

woman, abortion, whore, murderer,
obviously no saint, there's only one other
woman, madonna, prostitute,
take your choice keep your baby,
the rain falls so finely that it almost shimmers like a heat
haze,
the other day-long abortion intake women;
embarrassed, scared, ashamed, resigned,
hiding behind their curtain,
i drew one side of mine back,
i am here,
i have had an abortion before,
this is my second one,
i do not want your sympathy which tells me it's wrong but
poor you we'll forgive you,
i want your acceptance,
i do not take this lightly,
the nurses say nothing except that my brother cannot stay
with me for five minutes,
i know where my bed is,
i know the drill,
what else can they have to say to me, disapproving eyes
misappointed lives,
she didn't know the drill the young woman opposite,
she asked me,
i know,
we are not worthy of their attention,
this is london,
this is city living,
no warmth, no love, no, no,
black woman all we and they.
blood on my hands as i write,
blood up my back and down my thighs,
i ask for a fresh sheet and a fresh pad,
the old are both stained a dark red,
as i move for the sheet to be pulled out my pad slips and
blood deep rich red

pours like rain and tears onto the old sheet.
i felt the anaesthetic burn in my vein sending pain like
    sparks of fire up my arm
then hazy, out, to awaken in more pain,
knives shredding my womb,
my legs are hot in this bed and aching,
but i cannot move too much for fear the blood will pour
    again,
the nurses have warmed with familiarity,
i am relieved — and i am numb
before i went into theatre my hand on my belly, i said
    goodbye,
now the loss is physical pain and through a blank there are
    tears.
day after — is today,
i dreamt last night about my baby, my baby girl ella,
i breast fed her,
brought her back to life, when shrivelled she looked like the
    black plastic dolls of my childhood,
bathed, sang to her, talked with her,
took endless joy in my child,
woke up happy tried to explain my dream,
smelling the fresias and watching the brilliance of the
    daffodils and tulips in the windowlight,
i woke up elated, you see,
i was getting up to see my baby,
who isn't.

The women could be
invisible . . .

Blood Women

◆◆◆◆◆◆◆◆◆◆◆◆◆◆◆◆◆◆◆◆◆◆◆◆◆◆◆◆◆◆◆◆◆◆◆◆

Roma Thomas

Woman, blood makes you the outsider
makes you wait,
cast down your eyes in shame.
Wear that bell around your neck, cry unclean unclean.
Woman in your blood prison
condemned by whispered curses,
don't touch him, don't touch them, don't touch that.
Barred from the holy temple,
Once they say,
    "A woman disobeyed
    went to pray while she was in blood
    knelt before a shining altar
    offered up her sacrifice, swaying
    a sweet well fatted calf
    consumed in a mountain of red gold flame.
    When she turned around they swear they saw
    a red mark upon her forehead,
    blood red burning shame
    Woman in blood Woman in shame
    Woman, wailing, wailing.
    Hatred and Fear stormed,
    Merciless they dashed away the cup of salvation
    from her lips".
The gentle priest spat in her face
the pious worshippers struck out with their fists
they drove her from that place, into the dust
the holy men took up arms against the bloody intrusion
they feared the blood
abhorred the womb
their stony hearts bore a brutal witness against blood
    women.
Blood Sisters we knelt in the dust, prayed, touched the
    Divinity.

Whispered curses echoed around the temple
piteous cries of the condemned
but Blood Women we uplifted our voices
in silvered dresses dancing our worship
making music of our spirits
purified by our blood
Women in blood casting off the mark of shame.
Women in love.

Mutilation

◆◆◆

Shabnam

Early morning
The sun is still young
soon to rise to full glory
maturity
The girl-child is still young yet to grow to full glory

But no it is not to be allowed
her spirit is never to be free
she is to be crushed.

The sun is shining
the girl-child is woken
taken to a sunless place.
There are many women there
Love
Uncertainty
bewilderment
fear
terror
the screams fill the air.

They have wounded you
Cut out a part of you
I can never replace
I want to see the moon shining in your eyes

We must stop this sister
Together
It must end
Never again
never.
But see the sun is rising again
over another girl-child
My sister.

Mombasa Old Town

Bernardine Evaristo

Dry heat and dusty roads line the Old Town
narrow alleys and tightly packed houses.
Glimpsed through trees the Indian Ocean.
Its winds cooling this tropical heat.
Men sell Cassava chips wrapped in paper,
spiced with chilli-salt and lemon
and the smells of the fish markets
the meat markets stench the air.

Mango skins rot by the way.

Matatu's honk and hoot their way
through the town with young men
hanging from the doors shouting
their destinations: Nyali!
                Likoni!
                Malindi!

Old men walk slow . . . sure . . . steady
Kanga-clad, grey curls close cropped,
whilst all men haunt the streets like flies.
Everywhere; they are everywhere.

Caught dissapearing around corners,
women in Purdah billow their way
like black ghosts fading
for the women could be invisible here.
The women could be invisible.

Where do I go.
Who do I turn to . . .

Sister

Shabnam

When the rest of the world
is one big weapon
firing at me
sometimes missing sometimes hitting
When the ground opens
under my feet
and I smash my bangles
in despair and defeat
You take me into your
familiar inviting arms
and gently wash my bloodied wrists
and try to love the pain away.
You cook me Saag and Maki Ki Roti
and put Mhendi on my feet
You tell me silly jokes in punjabi
and dance a bhangara for me
You know what to do
sister
because you are me
and you have felt my pain
You can make me forget and laugh and hope.
But sister
where do I go
who do I turn to
when you
turn against me.
When you rip open the wounds
you once healed.
Sister you have seen my scars
you have felt my pain
and you have seen me bleed.
Before you I am raw
naked

open
to your love
and your hate.
Women you can destroy me
but sister ultimately
it is suicide
for I am you
we are one

An Open Letter

Carmen Tunde

Dear Risparl,
Jaswinder
Hazel
Perminder
It hasn't been easy
loving you.

After all
I was taught
you were a different species
and somewhat superior

After all
Your hair was straight
like the whites
nearer to God

Your people went from
brown to beige,
mine right down to black
Yuch!

Your nose wasn't flat
Your hair wasn't wild
Asian people's family
were strong and together
Asian people
had never
been SLAVES.

You called me
Bunderiyah — monkey
and laughed

In Southall
you owned a lot of shops
ran surgeries, dentists,
lawyers and opticians!

My stepdad said
I must never go to your
cinema again.

After all
Your people were plenty
in trinidad
and in all the best jobs.

Mind you, Ulyn
cooked the best roti
I've ever tasted
West Indian roti
that is.

A lot of her family
were East Asian

She was proud of that
she could call her
African man,
a nigger
when she felt like it.
And she did.

The system made sure
it was a long time
before I knew
that you were enslaved too.

And by the British.
That's how come we were all here
in white man's land.

You had darker skinned
people than me!
And I didn't know that
most of you worked
in factories too.

Yeh. And the whites said
our food smelled bad too!
In fact they'd 'like' us
coz we spoke English
and wore skirts and trousers,
And 'liked' you coz
you had a culture
of your own!

For control,
you know, in a way
we had the same enemy!

Yeh, in fact, we were
all dirty coons,
wogs or coolies.
Darkies and blackies

Nignogs and mammies

We all had a back home
of hot sun, fruit trees
and poverty.
Jesus, we had so much
in common.
'Backward!'
'Underdeveloped'.

I had swallowed
so much of it
about me
about you.

It was good to start
spewing up the rot
bit by bit.

I am sixteen
and see brothers
parading with
the skinheads
'paki-bashing'

WHAT'S GOING ON!!?!?

Gurdip singh Chaggar
was murdered by whites,
they said — one down, one million to go.

Racist attack,
Racist attack!

At twenty-two years
I see
'Unite and Fight'
'Black people are here to stay'
'Free George Lindo'

'Southall Black Sisters'
'Free the Bradford 12'
'Organisation of Women of Asian and African Descent'

Black people
Black women
We are together
and strong.

How together?
How strong?

Afro-Asian Unity?
A stormy lesbian relationship,
close and challenging.
And yet
I don't want to be in the
minority again.
Neither do you.

What are we both afraid of?

Silenced...

◆◆

Avril Rogers-Wright

I fear that this door
will be shut at my face
with a resounding slam.
That you, you and you and you
black woman
would forgo your power
to write
retell your, our history
without distortions
or hiding where we came from
or where we are heading for.

Writing is no fickle tool
imaginery
its a real existing line
the continuation of our histories
by ourselves
to be passed on from child to child
generation to generation
each lengthen the line
in as much truth as possible.

For once one has the power
to write
and is false with it
oppression will reign stronger
our struggles mocked
in this kind of denial of aspects of ourselves.

No One Has Time For My Uncertainties

Sylvia Parker

No one has time for my uncertainties
No one has time for my fears . . .

I would like one quiet afternoon
To peel away the layers of doubt
which cover me
Metamorphosise into some jewel
Become some summer saxaphone note
and rise and fall on a warm breeze
Fading slowly, painlessly, beautifully away

. . . the warm comforting shoulder I expect
never materialises
I am left with granite and steel
The pool of light which could be my salvation
Is forever engrained with dust
I choke as the particles reach my lungs
I find that the thing I thought would save me
Is the cause of my greatest despair

No one has time for my uncertainties
                    time for my fears
I am quickly judged and then discarded
Not given time to materialise
Whole.

Contradictions

Carmen Tunde

How are we to understand
the extreme cruelty of human life, black sisters?
Is it with tolerance and
philosophical knowingness?

Can we really blame the new men
for the lies they were told by the old men?
Can we really blame the new whites
for the lies they were told by the old whites?
Anymore than
blaming the women for lies told
and retold between us?
Anymore than blaming the black and brown
for the lies retold between us?

Has not a consciousness grown,
a collectivity?
Am I not a black lesbian
self-defined and knowing myself
where before I was a stranger?
Was not Grenada a socialist land?
And Cuba still.
Are not the women organising?

Have I not chosen to be free
where my mother still suffers
the terror of man-violence,
the pain of work-violence
and self-negation?

But am I to talk of a calm tolerance,
a calm tolerance!
A quiet acceptance!
When all around me

hunger is rife,
degradation and strife!

I cry and I cry
for we black girls whose bodies
and minds are raped
from as young as babies.

I cry and I cry
for we black women who grow up
to work in the factory or the hospital
servicing still for the pennies to feed the children,

I cry for we black people
and people of colour
who have kept our dignity
in the face of genocide.

I cry for the white women
whose bitter taste of racism
lines my mouth;
who still service their men
even as they long
for us to service them.

I weep at the white man
who holds the responsibility
in his monster mind
for the imminent destruction
of a whole planet;
whose penis fetish;
whose mirror magnetism
reaks of and carries
putrifying violation on our heads.

Stone cold anger is mine
where I stand ice-still
only my eyes following
showing the burning fire of rage

within
One move and my body and spirit
leap fluid into action,
my legs and arms hold
the collective power
of black women,
and if they swing and contact
tall buildings will fall
so the shell of man could only
crumble.

Contradictions!

If all my oppressors were destroyed
there would be few left on this earth.
Yet if we are to teach
we must learn tolerance.
My life is one long containment
My life is one long containment!

I can only describe the violence
I've visualised blasting on others
in self-defence.

I can only write or sing
the pain I feel.

Could a black lesbian,
defined minority within a minority,
within a minority within a minority,
show her majority wisdom?

Has not a consciousness grown,
a collectivity?
Was not Grenada a socialist land?
And Cuba still?
Are not the women organising?

Am I not a black lesbian
self-defined and knowing myself
where before I was a stranger?

The Song the Suicide Sings

Sylvia Parker

bruised and battered as i am
i attempt to create a poem for myself
i attempt to comfort myself
i attempt to see myself as valid
alongside so many other images

bruised and battered as i am
i attempt to make me smile with some word
i attempt to see myself as live
i attempt to see myself as valid
i attempt to throw off the death shroud

with no recognisable source
with no recognisable strength
i attempt to give my soul voice
i attempt to give my voice voice
i attempt to see myself as valid

the validity of my right to be
lies rooted in a child with no memory
the validity of my right to be
lies rooted in a shattered image
which it appears will not come to life

bruised and battered as i am
with no recognisable strength
i explore different alternatives
i attempt to give my voice voice
i attempt to give myself validity
alongside so many other images
i explore different alternatives
but with no recall
with no recognisable source
my voice falters and lies unformed

Today

Gabriela Pearse

A woman with a gash
so deep and wide in
her black soul
came and spilled her
self over me.

Asking to be held
like no-one held her

Asking to be fed
like no-one fed her.

She crawled beneath
my skirt trembling and
afraid and clasped
my life boat legs.

But I had meetings
to go to,
and a world to save.

A Bouquet Of Flowers

Avril Rogers-Wright

Let us pour GASOLINE down each others throats,
bringing forth guttering music.
Let us tug free each others innards,
so that the eagles can claw at the quivering mass.

Let us with insufferable arrogance,
hold on rigidly.
After all, my culture stayed intact!
My people never bowed!
When the flocks have dispersed,
singled out,
we know from those who,
have righteously taken upon themselves to judge,
careful labelling, parcelling and slotting.
Yes, don't we know the law of the streets.

Let us wage a revolution of definite divisions.
And those that do not quite come up to scratch,
shall face the firing squad.
Surely you know that these people are no longer
of any use to us.
In the last wispy smoke of the guns,
there will be less confusion.

The hyaenas laughter echoes in the jungle.
One day, we too will be able to share the joke.
Meanwhile let us be conscientious in developing
these traits.
And when the time is ripe,
we shall present the world,
with a bouquet of wilted flowers.

In the cold face of the birth of tomorrows dawn,
the hyaenas laughter is translated for us.
While the young idealist sobs in the corner.

Labels

◆◆

Zhana

Black, African,
nigger coloured coon darky
negro Afro American Black

If I'm Black and you're Asian ,
and she's Puerto Rican that makes us Third World
(But not Caribbean)

But you're black and you're Asian
so I must be African
but my mother's Black American

The Rastas are Africans
looked down on by Nigerians
Who won't talk to Westindian
Sons of Slaves

Black lesbian feminist womanist
radical separatist vegetarian socialist anarchist
fascist
labels labels labels labels

Black heterosexual sisters
Say Black lesbians
Should love men while
Black lesbians claim that
We don't love women
But our mothers are women.
Heterosexual
Black
Women

Sisters under the skin
Sisters under the skin
Sisters under the skin

Sisters of the skin

Nigger coloured coon darky
Animal bestial ugly dirty
Stupid ignorant backwards
Lazy insolent shiftless useless
Black American
Black as sin
Black American
Black Death
Black American
Black Hole
Black American

Christian
lesbian
socialist capitalist
working class
middle class
anarchist
labels labels labels labels

White lesbian radical feminist
vegetarian separatist
fascist fascist
labels labels labels labels

Atheist
heterosexual
born-again Rasta
upper-class lower-class
national anarchist
Anarchic nationalist
labels labels labels labels

Labels are wonderful things
They let us all know where we stand
Or fall

Crowning Glory

Zhana

My mom never had hair like mine.
Hers would fall naturally
Into tight curls, kinks and naps
If she didn't press Africa out of it.
Smell of hair burning, screaming in agony
Pressed into shape
Hanging limply
Soulectomised.

My mom never had hair like mine.
She used to comb and brush my hair for hours,
Pleased with herself for giving birth
       to a head like mine.
She washed it lovingly,
Up to her elbows in dirty suds.
"You have such *beautiful* hair!" she'd crow,
"Your hair is your crowning glory."
She squeezed it, stroked it,
Caressed it, wrapped her hands in it,
Ran her fingers through it,
Rubbed it up and down.

I didn't get on with most of the girls at school.
Didn't know why.
"They're just jealous of your hair", Mom would say.
I never believed her.
Years later, I found out
       she was right.
My hair hung down in
Two straight braids.
They annoyed me when
They fell over my shoulders,
So I tossed them back
       with abandon.

The other girls looked at me
With malice in their hearts.
"She's showing off again", they thought,
As I tossed my braids about.
They resented so much
Hair they'd never have,
"Gooood hair",
Contrasted with their African heads.

I envied the girls
with "nigger naps".
They automatically had something in common.
A bond
I could never share.
They were always braiding
And fussing
And straightening and perming,
But my hair was just "there",
Not white,
But not quite Black.

"Don't ever cut your hair", Mom's voice comes down to me
      through the years.
"It's your crowning glory.
Girls will try
To get you to cut your hair
Because they're jealous.
They'll say,
'You'd look nice with short hair,
I know a pretty style.' "
I never believed her,
But years later,
I found out she was right.

Mother never told me
About the men
Who hankered after a white woman
with a Black face.

Who talked to my hair
Not to me.
Who longed for long hair
Across their pillows.
Who saw the hair on my head
And reasoned that
The hair on my pussy
Must be silk.
She only told me
That women would be jealous,
And years later,
I found out she was right.

Laughter

Bekleen Leong

i
When I laugh
It is a bubbling rebellion
(Like bouillon)
The way it pops out and bursts the air
Volcanic eruption
and dies down
oozing lava
down my blushing dimpled cheeks.

A poem
is like a joke —
not always serious
(and sometimes even funny).

ii
Years of vicious anger
and hating everyone who didn't understand you
(Which was 99 + 1% of people)
Building up into an uncontrollable
frothy lava
of laughter:

Hysterical you might think
Only now
quite controlled
set into a repressed giggle
or a squashed smirk;
my laughter is not the sort to move mountains,
But rather just enough
to allow some sleep at night.

Being a lesbian . . .

The Coming-Out Welcome

Avril Rogers-Wright

For The Blacklesbian Support Network

To those that have come.
Remember
our laughter
rich and bubbly in us
our open doors
chinwagging from the window.

I want you to come
to the warmth
positive selves Blackwomeness
to know a solace
before
meeting the wolves in sheep's clothing

To know that you came
a lasting memory
of beautiful flowers
that you are or were
one of us
before teething to bloom
in your new home.

Lesbian

Meiling Jin

Being a lesbian
means being myself
kissing your smooth
dark skin of an evening
and loving you.
In you I see myself:
deep pools of strength
and softness
washed over by a rising tide;
it covers our form
then ebbs away
and we remain,
as we always were.

Being a lesbian
means fighting hard
against an ever encroaching poster
of a man and a woman holding hands.
The poster explodes
into a million fragments
and a fine dust descends
and settles in my brain.
The door bell rings
and it's the gas man,
who calls me,
Mrs Ching Chang Chong
and enquires where
my husband is.

My family know
I have no husband,
only a lover
who is a woman;

such things
they've never heard of.
My sister fears
I may gobble up
her children,
this pains me.

Being myself
isn't easy
but being someone else
would be harder
now that I've swum
in the sea of passion
and felt *my* strength
and *my* softness.
I have known your lips
and your embrace
I feel alive

ain't I just.

The Women Loving Women

Shabnam

The women loving women
bear no name
and wear no badges
The women loving women
are everywhere
so beware
   Do you see the women
in the blood red sari
and mahendi on her feet
   Do you see the women
with the long locks
and the haughty walk
   Do you see the women
with the deep laughter lines
on her face
and a child on her hip
They are
Everywhere
Bearing no names
wearing no badges
an underground army
with no uniforms
and no weapons
except love
for women
Beware.

While your face uncoiled
its questioning arc against
the sky . . .

I Saw You Sad

Dinah Butler

I saw you sad
long and long
to gravity you stretched
and held releasing slowly into
your egg curve contemplation.
An arm recovered to pull,
to pull and raise, unfold
from the viscous pain you held
while your face

uncoiled its questioning arc
against the sky
to bruise the cloud line grey
before sinking,
furrowing your brows crested
down to where your mouth
tipped parted, vacant
with forgotten breathing.

Sun's First Rising

M. Ayio

To open eyes
With hope
For a bright and beautiful yellow globe,
The sun's first rising,
Enhanced, perhaps,
By an embryo
Of soft fluffy down.

But reality
Turns blind belief
To dreary disappointment.

The morning cracked, unwillingly,
Leaking a grey,
Sordid corruption
That hurt
The eye
To see.

Summer

Dinah Butler

Sunshine, a sister,
Creeps sly under the door.
So rich,
She bursts in with the frankness of butter.
Another immodest morning,
Eager in the wings
As the birds first throat her approach.
And the nervous wind wants to pour cold scorn
But legs it to safety and hovers,
A shy adolescent breeze until safely evening
When he ruffles up proud
And stalks the silent gap between
The edges of her rule.

A rolled yawn-tipped afternoon,
Pollen heavy, buzzes dusky, full bloated like bees,
Striped industrious berries that float heavy.
Sunshine, a sister,
Gathers up and strides over the hill.
The sky blushes up bashful as she passes,
Keeps darkened blue eyes long lifted
Not believing her gone.

Don't fear mi dear
you are loved . . .

Old Wisdom

◆◆

Shabnam

There is
an old Indian story
which says
that if you love someone
then let her go.
If she returns
she was meant
for you
If she does not
then
she was never yours
so I say to you
sweet women
fly away
and may you find love
with whom
you were meant to
and may the sun
always shine on you

Just Thinking...

◆◆◆

Patricia Hilaire

The flame flickers again as I sit
thinking of calling you
the flame warms me as you are not here
in my thoughts you bring warmth inside of me
and knowing you're not far pleases me

Wanting to be with you
as you create on paper
with a brush that is a pen
and words that are your paints

Inspiration that does not just come from the sea
but from your life and all of us
who are part of your life

Maybe you sit in almost silence . . .
with the wind beating against your window
and the sound of a bus passing
every fifteen minutes . . .

Are you sitting at your table?
which is now a desk
for the hours that you sit and write
with thick yellow sox on your feet
to keep your toes warm
and rainbows hugging your sweet smelling
body round and round and . . .

Is your mind at peace as you paint?
do you paint a story?
or some lines of poetry?

I love you sweet woman
but fear this love I have in me for you
for I do not want to be the thought that

causes you to lose sleep
nor the thorn in your skin
that causes you pain

But you have opened sealed doors
and boxes of well preserved memories
memories that needed care and loving in
handling
you have treated my wounds and left me
able to care for self again
and in those boxes I now have you well sealed in,
in my secret places . . .

The flame flickers again as I sit here
thinking of calling you
thinking . . .
just thinking
thinking of calling you . . .

The Flower

Carmen Tunde

I like
to touch
the flower
between
your legs,
the petals
opening up
and sliding
my fingers
through your
warm
wet
nectar.

Movements

Bernardine Evaristo

Your face cupped
beneath my hands
reassuring

Your body shivers
at my touch
exciting

Your pelvis moves
slow sensual
circling

Your thighs smooth
hot power
turning

Your long shape
curves round
prowling

Your breasts brush
mine a whisper
calling

Your lips search
mine expectant
devouring

Our limbs in movement
compelling enriching

Our bodies together
opening delivering

Ameland

Bernardine Evaristo

The white ridged waves
surveyed at a distance
along the wide expanse of shoreline

There is time enough to know the waters,
time enough to close the gap
between the sea and me
as I sit and watch the waves
expanding my vision.
For the wind to blow askew
my newly forming locks that now
rise to the wind as the sea surges
forwards. I smile as you rush out
to meet the waves, then return, coming
nearer and nearer and I to welcome
you as you shape my hug.

I look over your shoulder
the sea watches and waits
knowing that very soon I return
to love the waves, the power of their
pull so much stronger than your form
as you hold me close; whilst
I give the little
that does not belong to this sea.

Secretes

Meiling Jin

Your breasts curve down
And then, at the last minute,
Turn up:
A very endearing feature.
I like to lay my head
And feel the rise and fall
Of your breathing
As you lie sleeping
Black hair
On dark skin;
My oozing
Snoozing
Darling
Chickadee
Dream on.
Our secrets lie safe,
Locked in the rhythm
Of your breathing.

For Sandra

◆◆

Shabnam

I want to lick that grin off your face
sweet woman
and taste your moist tangrine tongue
in my mouth
I want to reach out and touch
your swaggering body
and feel the rhythm change
I want to hold you in my arms
your soft warm breasts
rubbing against mine as
your cinnamon scented breath
quickens in my ears.
I want to move my fingers
down
the deep velvet ridge in your back
and up
strong weak thighs
I want to delve
into your spicy, sticky, lifegiving
folds
and smell the slow, fast
shuddering of your body
as you cling to me.

Because

Shabnam

when I cried
she thought
there was something in my eye
when I hurt
she asked
if I had indigestion
when I bled
she would not see
and when I said
I need
she walked away
and now
I no longer cry or hurt or bleed
I no longer need
I am emotionally aneamic
All systems shut down
and she says
please love me
why dont you love me?
and I say
Because.

Patricia

Gabriela Pearse

You deserve
the stars and
the aching moon
should be yours
to cradle
in velvet black skin
that glows as it
holds, rocks,
brings back to life
Womanspirit, that grows
as you water it
with your tears
and love
and care.

You deserve it all
to yourself
to me
bewitching enticing
to the security of
your gaze.

Don' fear mi dear
you are loved.

Summer Breeze

Dorothea Smartt

You bring:
songs to my lips
about sweet-soft-sensous . . .
you
who wraps herself about me
whose caress can be like a whisper
yet still creams me
whose air and vibrations draw me
who moves beautifully in her silent strength
whose light fingers tripping anywhere
on my skin
can release tides of desire in me.

Dream Sequence

Bernardine Evaristo

Watching your face in the dim light of your room
as you talk or sleep and rest.
Dreaming the day that the thin grey veil
which is held up between you and I will melt
into insignificance and that your loveliness
will weave intricate designs upon my body;
wanting my hands to trace the lines of war
embedded in your forehead.
stroke out the pain . . . kiss away the worry

for you have played deeply upon my heart
lightened my heart until I am intoxicated
by you . . . belly-soft . . . belly woman . . . belly-soft-beauty

and yet hung heavy as now, tonight I tread
warily on stones. Stones in a grey bay.
Blindfold at night and water.
Not wanting the difference
to be that which seperates.
listening to the wind make ripples . . . make ripples.

One day, maybe this day, I hope to be more energy
and less effort for you. Dreaming to be a gift of joy
a presence of magnificence, that you deserve.
To watch time pass into substance. Night into day's.

Your face sculpted by the moonlight.
Yet for me to unleash the gentleness
that you inspire.

Come lie, rest by me, you belly-soft . . .
belly-woman . . . belly-soft-beauty.
learning to love this cold winter.
Belly-soft....................beauty.

This Cat

Gabriela Pearse

This cat
she expects love.
Demands it
stalks it
feels she has a right to it.
She is not ashamed —
I wish I were more like this cat.

Sistahs

◆◆

Gabriela Pearse

. . . And four five six
different coloured black
women gathered together
to share
our treasures.
We sat a ring
we put food in the middle
we started around.

Each gave
we were there —
not in our shyness
not in our histories
not in keeping any games up
Each gave
her utter presence that
rare bird that alights
once in a black full dark blood moon.

Each gave
complete hearing —
we heard so hard
we were in danger of becoming one.
Letting each other in
was exciting
we were excited
    and bubbling
    — connected.

We talked black-woman-talk
all the different sides of it
We were so loud
we laughed
    slapped thighs

hooted and chortled
into the night.

We spoke the words
our mothers divided
                insane
                drunk and
                silenced
could not speak,
— boy we had centuries of
catchin' up to do.

Letting us share their pain
                and questions upon questions
                never asked —
they were watching us
sitting right behind us
slightly bewildered —
a bit shocked . . .
but smiling in their hearts.

A Poem For Black Women

Patricia Hilaire

Rarely has a door opened and said welcome
never has a crack been big enough
but through the crack
we see an endless boundary of another place

we will not wait to be allowed entry
that, we will seek on our own
for we know where the light does not shine
our spirit will glow
and where mist move on low ground
our spirit will take flight

The fire that burns on within us
is as strong as the wind on the eastern side
of the cliff
we know that the reflection will not move
when we come face to face with it
for we know that we must go where it is that
our soul desires

We will not be restricted
it is not a crime to say NO,
nor is it a crime to be in the presence
of self, taking control
and not being controlled
for what ever it is that we
black women desire
shall be ours to hold . . .

Contributors

Adjoa Andoh

Ghanaian/English Blackwoman. Born in Bristol 1963 1st child to Jacqui & Frank. Grew up in Bristol, Leeds, Wickwar & Wotton-Under-Edge, Glos. with brother Yeofi. Studied law for a year and a half at Bristol Polytechnic. Moved to London 1984 am now an actor, singer, writer. Lover of woman and womanspirit — all my best breaks have been through women! Live in Brixton with my wonderful daughter Jesse, whom I love best of all! Also Richard, Nicky, Jackie, Dorothea, Gabriella, Joanna, La, Nona, Bryony, John, Philip, Lola, Deb'bora, Sally, dancing, books, films, food, shoes, music.

M. Ayoi

I'm 31, born in the Caribbean but have lived here for 29 years. I am single and have no children. My main interest is the continued spiritual and artistic development of black women in this country.

Dinah Anuli Butler

Dinah Anuli Butler was born in 1960 to an English mother and an absent Nigerian father. She grew up in Barking, taught in Kenya for two years after finishing school and studied social anthropology at Sussex University. She has had poems published in West Africa magazine, Spare Rib, Women's Review and Tears in the Fence. She has finished her first collection of poems which is as yet unpublished. She works full-time, teaches writing workshops occasionally and is expecting her first child in March.

Zeina Carrington

Me Zeina Carrington, a 26 year old from Lebanese, Portuguese, French, Italian, and Trinidadian stock! Work with the mentally distressed in Hackney. I spend my 'precious' time writing, singing and travelling solo to far off challenging places in search of enlightenment and rampant adventure. I have written poetry for as long as I can recall which read as autobiographical landmarks and carthasis. Until recently these have remained private in contrast to my mother's published success in The Lebanon; although she committed suicide in 1979. I now permanently live in England, exiled from family in the Lebanon and minus parents. However, I have a younger sister who makes up for all in all ways imaginable!

Dr. Debjani Chatterjee

Born in Delhi, India. Educated in Japan, Bangladesh, India, Hong Kong, Egypt and the UK. Since 1984: Principal Community Relations Officer with the Sheffield Council for Racial Equality. Previously: Sector Manager in Marketing with British Steel Corporation. Also taught in schools, colleges and adult education in Manchester and Sheffield. Actively involved in various voluntary organisations. Management Committee member of: Sheffield Association for Voluntary Teaching of English, Radio Sheffield Advisory Council, Sheffield Non-statutory Co-ordinating Group, etc. Author of *Religion in A Passage to India* published by *Writers Workshop*, Calcutta, 1984. She also writes children's stories and draws occasional cartoons.

Bernardine Evaristo

I was born in 1959. My mother is English and my father is of the Yoruba of Nigeria. I work in theatre, essentially as a playwright and a tutor of Drama and of Writing for Theatre. My plays for Theatre of Black Women include: *'Tiger Teeth Clenched Not To Bite'*, *'Silhouette'* and *'Pyeyucca'*. The latter two were co-written with Patricia Hilaire. I traverse and travel for knowledge and insight and the ensuing perspective that is gained and which I aim to impart through my writing. Some of my poems are in the lesbian poetry anthology *'Beautiful Barbarians'* (ONLYWOMEN PRESS).

Patricia Hilaire

Born in London 1960 of caribbean parentage. In 1982 was instrumental in the setting up of Theatre of Black Women with Bernadine Evaristo. Plays written to date include *'As deep as the ocean sea'* (82) *'Just Another Day'* (82) *'Silhouette'* (83) *'Pyeyucca'* (84) the latter two were co-written with B. Evaristo and toured nationally. Her main area of work includes writing, performing tutoring and administration. "Trapped words have from time to time flowed from me, involuntarily at times to created both poetry and drama".

Meiling Jin

My star sign is Capricorn with Scorpio rising. I was born in Guyana and came to England when I was eight. I've written about this in the introduction to my book, *"Gifts from my Grandmother"* (SHEBA), and also in *The Funky Black Women's Journal*. I live in London now and am committed to fighting all forms of racism and sexism particularly in the media. I teach women's self defense and like writing for children.

Jackie Kay

I was born in Edinburgh in 1961. I was brought up in Glasgow. I've had poems published in *A Dangerous*

Knowing: Four Black Women Poets (SHEBA) *and Angels of Fire Radical Poetry Anthology* (CHATTO) I've had short stories published in *Everyday Matters 2* (SHEBA) and *Stepping Out* (PANDORA) I wrote my first play for Theatre of Black Women, *Chiaroscuro* which did the rounds between Feb-May of 86. At the moment I'm trying to write a novel which I hope to have finished before the end of this century.

Bekleen Leong

Born in Johannesburg in 1959. Brought up in a London suburb, lived in Brighton, France and Ireland for a while, came to London in 1984, where I got involved in the black women's movement. I am presently involved in compiling two books. One on immigrant Lesbians, and one of Chinese women in this country. I would like to spend more time writing. This is the first time my work has been published.

Sylvia Parker

Born 1963, London. Emigrated to Barbados aged 5, returned England 1975 to complete education. Hull university '82-'85, read Accounting. Currently working in a community project on a large south east London estate. Started writing at length 1982. Currently reviewing poetry produced over the last three years and attempting to finish lots of unfurnished short stories. Never published before. Also reviewing the chamelion inside, trying to decide whether to be part-time voluntary sector worker, part-time writer, sometime sage or full-time public sector accountant.

Gabriela Pearse

Grew up in Colombia-Chile-Switzerland-Grenada-Trinidad-England. I'm now living and working in London as a

Community Research Worker doing work around women's employment and training. I have a passion for humanity for discovering and digging up contradictions, differences and seeing how we can use these as sources of empowerment rather than conflict. I have been writing poetry and short stories for many years. I have poems published in *A Dangerous Knowing* (SHEBA) and have written a children's play with my mother which was performed by Theatre of Black Women Jan-April '87.

Avril Rogers-Wright

My name is Avril, I'm twenty three years old. At the moment, I've just started really living my life. About writing, for me it is a gift I'm blessed and cursed with. Through the support given by close friends and family, I have gained enough confidence to share my writing instead of hiding them in the wardrobe. I'm grateful to them for helping me to come to terms with my gift. I believe and promote that all women should use whatever creative power they have fully in order to document their lives which is a necessary herstory for young women — the future generation.

B. B. Samuel

B. B. Samuel is a very private person.

Shabnam

An Indian woman coming from a long line of stroppy Sikh women who only write when in love or depressed. Adores Sci fi, good food, good films and sleeping. Working in a video company at the present.

Dorothea Smartt

Africa — "Liberia", Daddy said.
Barbados.
Barbados — Mum's from The Ivy, Dad's from Henry's Lane.
Battersea — South London.
My Past — In my Mum's hands and my Dad's back.
   Thoughts, dreams, and spirits that made me after my
   mother/sistah. Apart, from all that, I feel the presence of
   Blackpeople in knowing myself, the sistahs especially . . .
My future — There is a BlackGoddess in me.
   She stirs, when you tap those memories of being, that are
   in all of us. BlackGoddess re-emerging
   sensing the erotic.

Roma Thomas

Aged 24 years. Started writing off and on a few years ago to
record my perspective of Black women's experience in
Britain, and write about these in a way that challenges
stereotypes. I am an Afro-Caribbean woman born in
England, currently working for a local authority.

Carmen Tunde

Learning to love myself as Black and mixed race girlchild
and Woman by searching out my place in history and
politics; organising for change with my different peoples;
supporting and being. Supported by sistas; expressing
myself through singing currently with *Sistahs In Song*,
drum with *I spirit*, piano, poetry, writing, dancing, aikido;
learning to take rest or else! Dragging myself out of a mire of
depression by believing it is possible and working at it;
embracing the positive vibrations through spirituality, my
candles my sacred place and images of my African Women
Ancestors and Goddesses. Thirty years and *still far* to go.

One Love. (PS *Sistahs in Song* can be booked through Box 28, 190 Upper St, London N1 1RQ)

Tina Wildebeest

I was born in Manchester (1950) of a white, British mother and Nigerian father. My parents never married, and as their relationship ended soon after I was born, I never met my father. I was brought up in a virtually all white, working class environment which, in terms of race, left me with a very confused sense of identity. This was one of the reasons my ten year marriage to a white guy broke down four years ago. I have been writing for about four years and I'm a member of Manchester's only Black Women's writing group.

Zhana

Zhana — I was born Cyndy Jennings, in New York City; I moved to London in 1982. My life's work is to facilitate Black women's recording our world as we see it and reshaping it as we want it to be. I often experience irritation, rage and fury because of what has been stolen from Black women, as well as what we continue to steal from each other. I have co-founded the Black Women's Writing Workshop and the *Funky Black Women's Journal*, and I am currently co-authoring/co-editing *Sojourn*, a book about relationships between Black women, to be published by METHUEN.

Editors

Da Choong

Born and brought up on an island in South East Asia, but have now spent more than half my life in England. I come from a long line of immigrants who travelled from China in search of work; I now have relatives in four continents and even more countries. Books are a particular passion of mine — which is why I am so pleased to have been involved in bringing this book out.

Olivette Cole-Wilson

I have been a member of Black Womantalk since it began in 1983. I have been a member of two women's writing groups and have been involved in various music projects over the years. I am really excited that at last our first publication has finally arrived.

Bernadine Evaristo

See contributors section

Gabriela Pearse

See contributors section